NICKELBACK
DARK HORSE

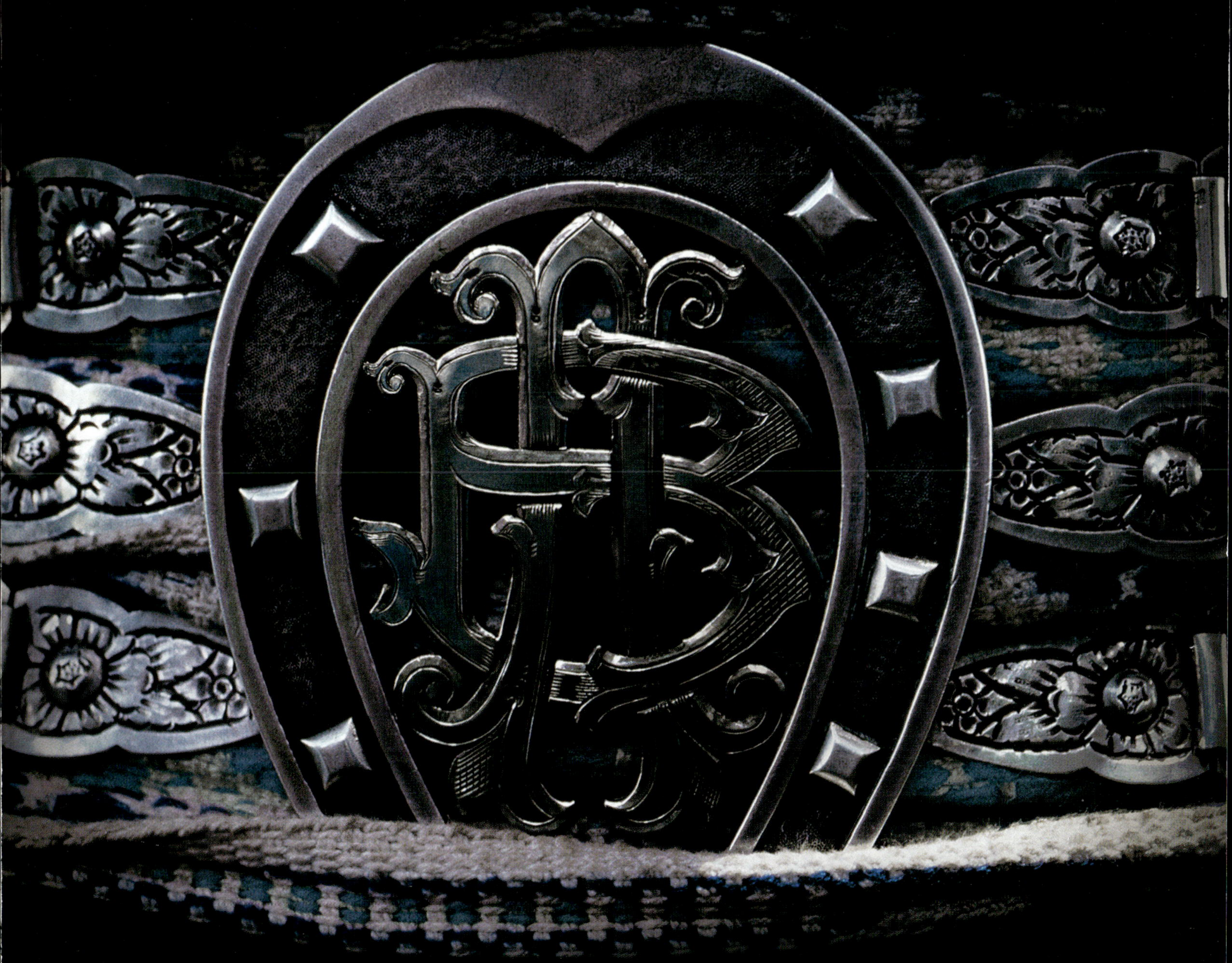

WWW.NICKELBACK.COM
WWW.ROADRUNNERRECORDS.COM

Management: Bryan Coleman for Union Entertainment Group

Album Artwork: © 2008 Roadrunner Records
Front Cover Image: © Corbis Corporation
Album Photography: Chapman Baehler

Alfred Publishing Co., Inc.
16320 Roscoe Blvd., Suite 100
P.O. Box 10003
Van Nuys, CA 91410-0003
alfred.com

Copyright © MMIX by Alfred Publishing Co., Inc.
All rights reserved. Printed in USA.

ISBN-10: 0-7390-5883-5
ISBN-13: 978-0-7390-5883-1

CONTENTS

SOMETHING IN YOUR MOUTH 5

BURN IT TO THE GROUND 15

GOTTA BE SOMEBODY 22

I'D COME FOR YOU 28

NEXT GO ROUND 34

JUST TO GET HIGH 41

NEVER GONNA BE ALONE 47

SHAKIN' HANDS 53

S.E.X. 64

IF TODAY WAS YOUR LAST DAY 73

THIS AFTERNOON 81

NICKELBACK

Chad Kroeger ~ Vocals & Guitars
Mike Kroeger ~ Bass
Ryan Peake ~ Guitar & Vocals
Daniel Adair ~ Drums & Vocals

SOMETHING IN YOUR MOUTH

Words and Music by
CHAD KROEGER, JOEY MOI
and MUTT LANGE

All gtrs. in Drop D, ⑥ = D

Moderately ♩ = 124

Something in Your Mouth - 10 - 3

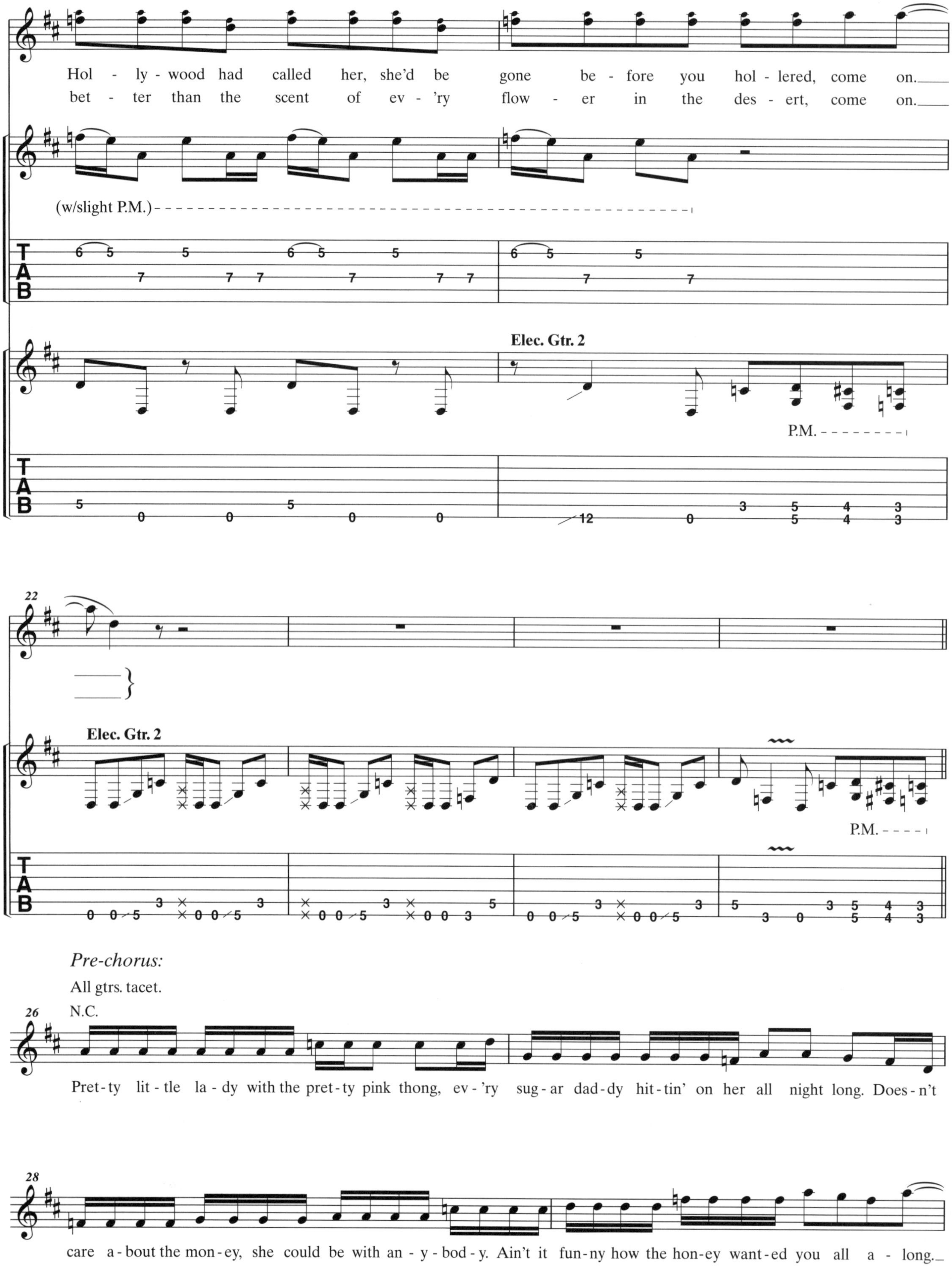
Hol - ly - wood had called her, she'd be gone be - fore you hol - lered, come on.
bet - ter than the scent of ev - 'ry flow - er in the des - ert, come on.
(w/slight P.M.)
Elec. Gtr. 2
P.M.
22
Elec. Gtr. 2
P.M.
Pre-chorus:
All gtrs. tacet.
26
N.C.
Pret - ty lit - tle la - dy with the pret - ty pink thong, ev - 'ry sug - ar dad - dy hit - tin' on her all night long. Does - n't
28
care a - bout the mon - ey, she could be with an - y - bod - y. Ain't it fun - ny how the hon - ey want - ed you all a - long.

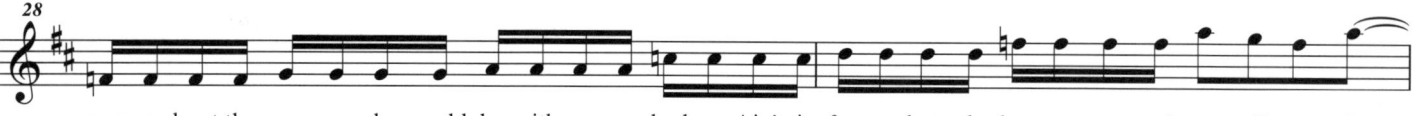

BURN IT TO THE GROUND

*All gtrs. in Drop D, down 1 1/2 steps:
⑥ = B   ③ = E
⑤ = F♯ ② = G♯
④ = B   ① = C♯

Lyrics by CHAD KROEGER
Music by NICKELBACK

Moderate shuffle ♩ = 124

*Recording sounds one and one half steps lower than written.

**Elec. Gtr. 1 dbld.

Verses 1 & 2:

mid - night, damn right, we're wound up too tight.
(2.) scream - in' like de - mons and swing - in' from the ceil - ing.

Rhy. Fig. 1
Elec. Gtr. 1

© 2008 WARNER-TAMERLANE PUBLISHING CORP., ARM YOUR DILLO PUBLISHING INC.,
BLACK DIESEL MUSIC, INC. and MOI MUSIC PRODUCTIONS INC.
All Rights Administered by WARNER-TAMERLANE PUBLISHING CORP.
All Rights Reserved

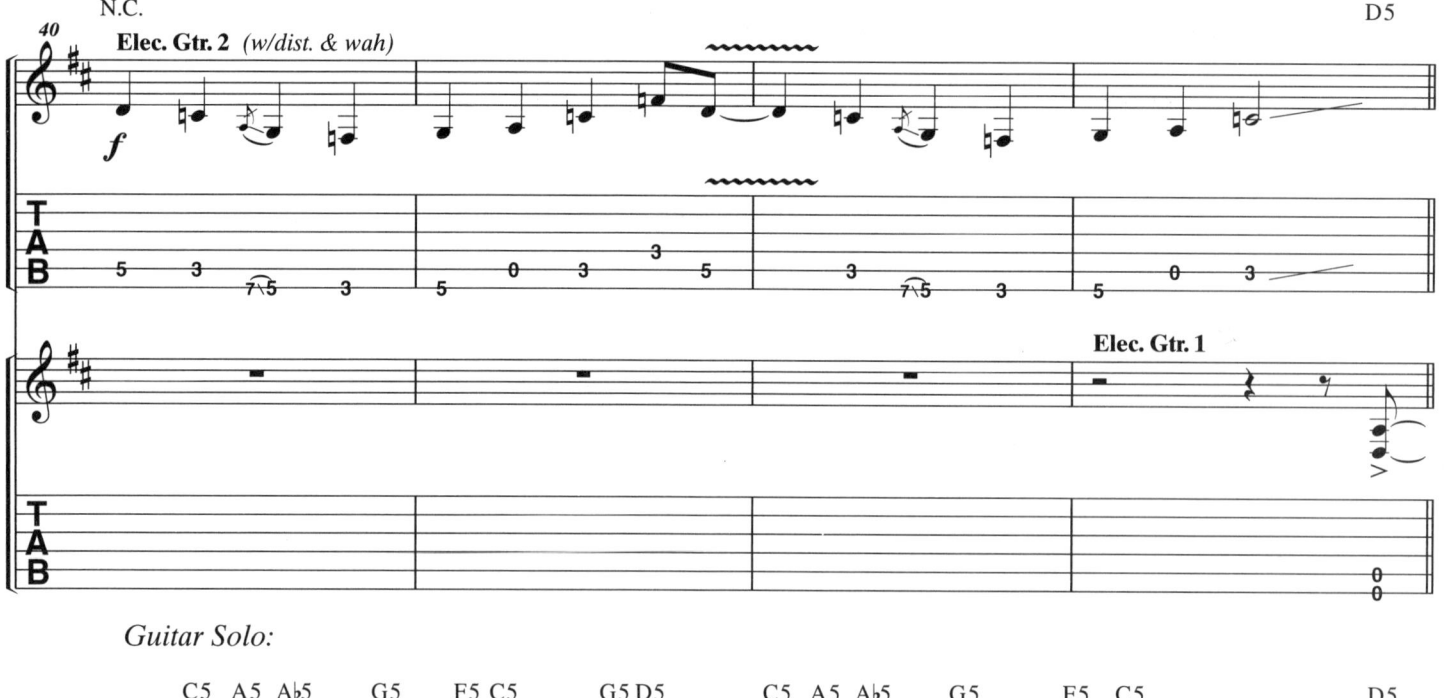

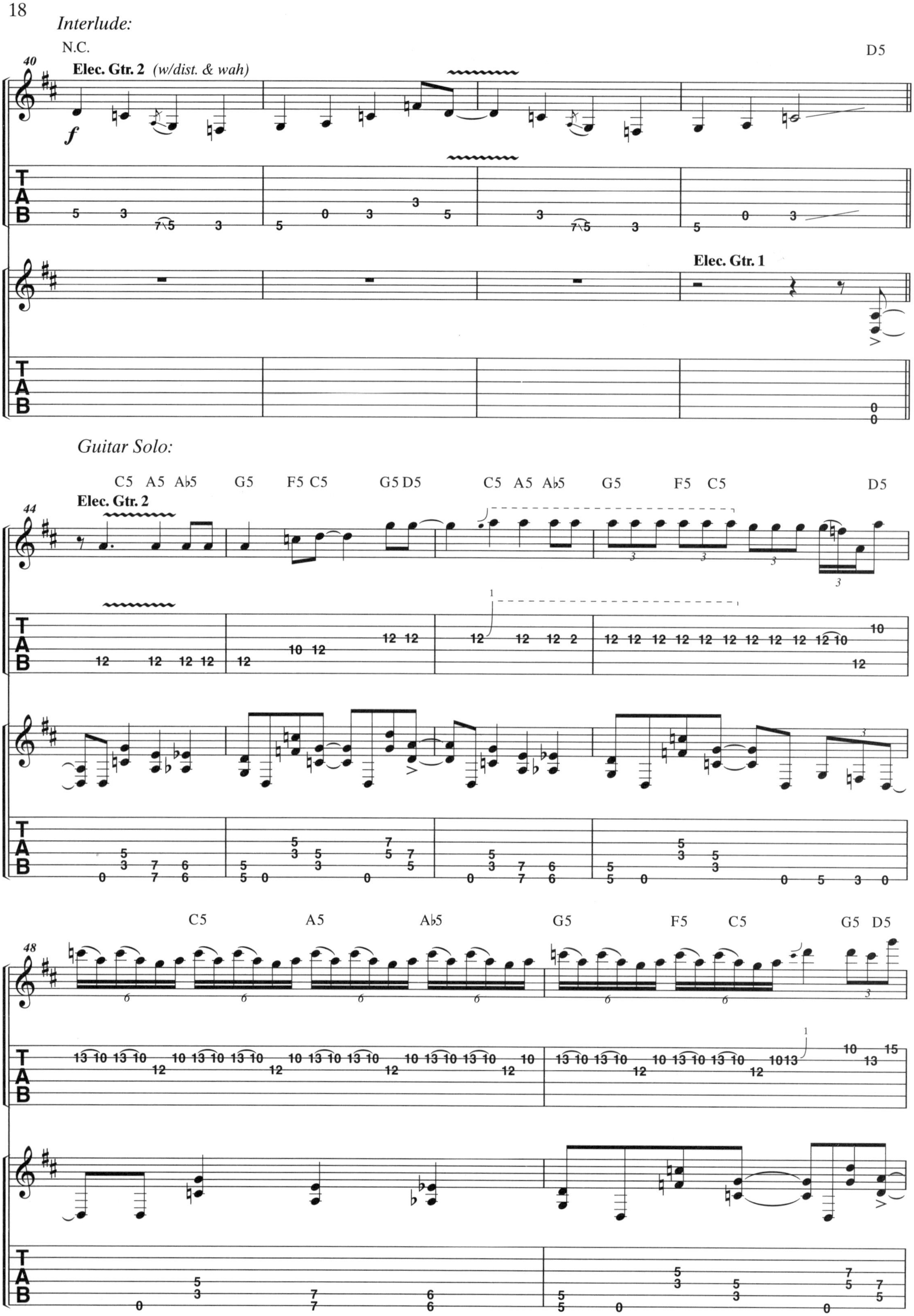
Interlude:
N.C.
D5
Elec. Gtr. 2 (w/dist. & wah)
f
Elec. Gtr. 1
Guitar Solo:
C5 A5 A♭5 G5 F5 C5 G5 D5 C5 A5 A♭5 G5 F5 C5 D5
Elec. Gtr. 2
C5 A5 A♭5 G5 F5 C5 G5 D5

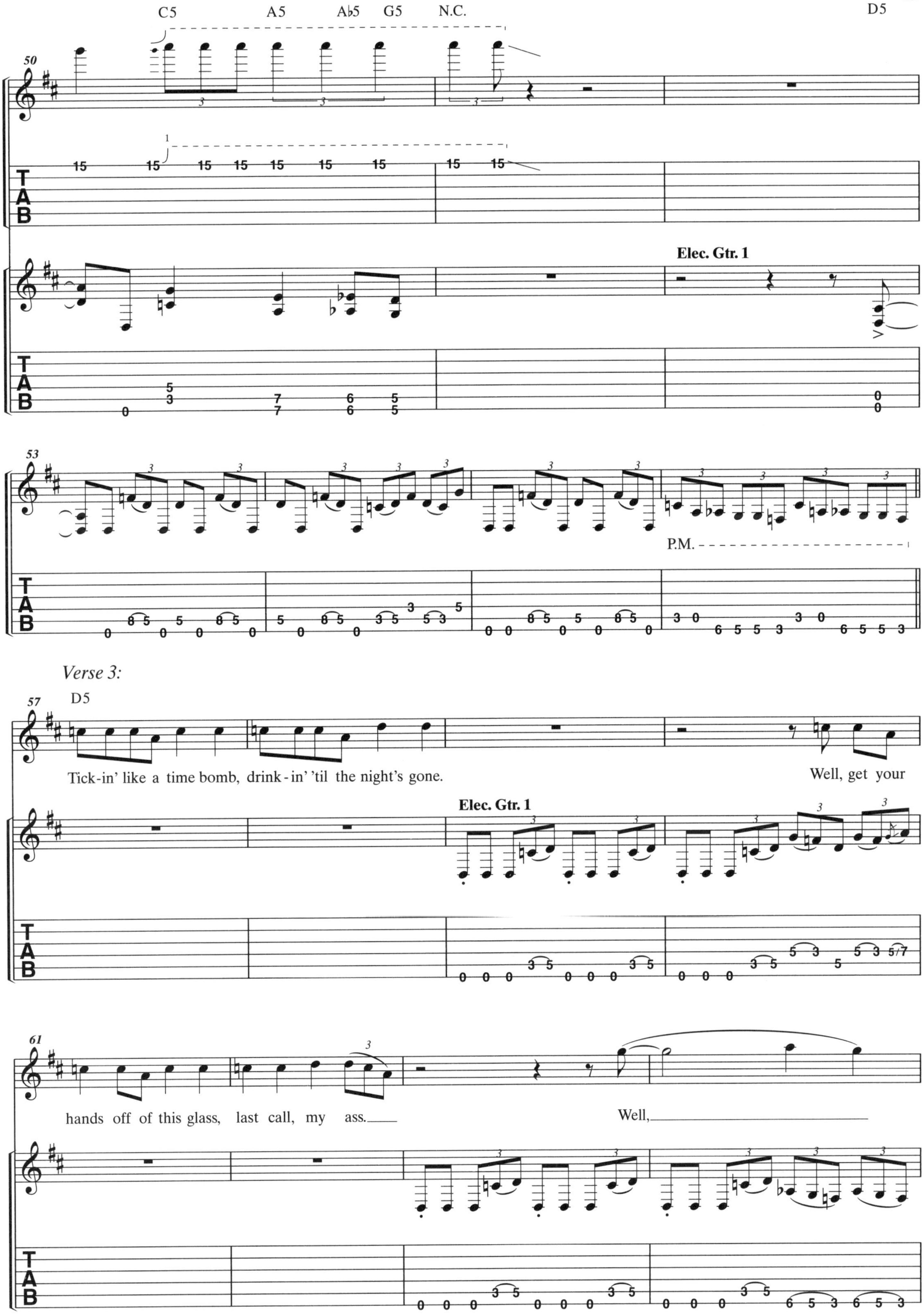
C5
A5
A♭5
G5
N.C.
D5
50
Elec. Gtr. 1
53
P.M.
Verse 3:
57
D5
Tick-in' like a time bomb, drink-in' 'til the night's gone.
Well, get your
Elec. Gtr. 1
61
hands off of this glass, last call, my ass.
Well,

GOTTA BE SOMEBODY

Lyrics by CHAD KROEGER
Music by NICKELBACK

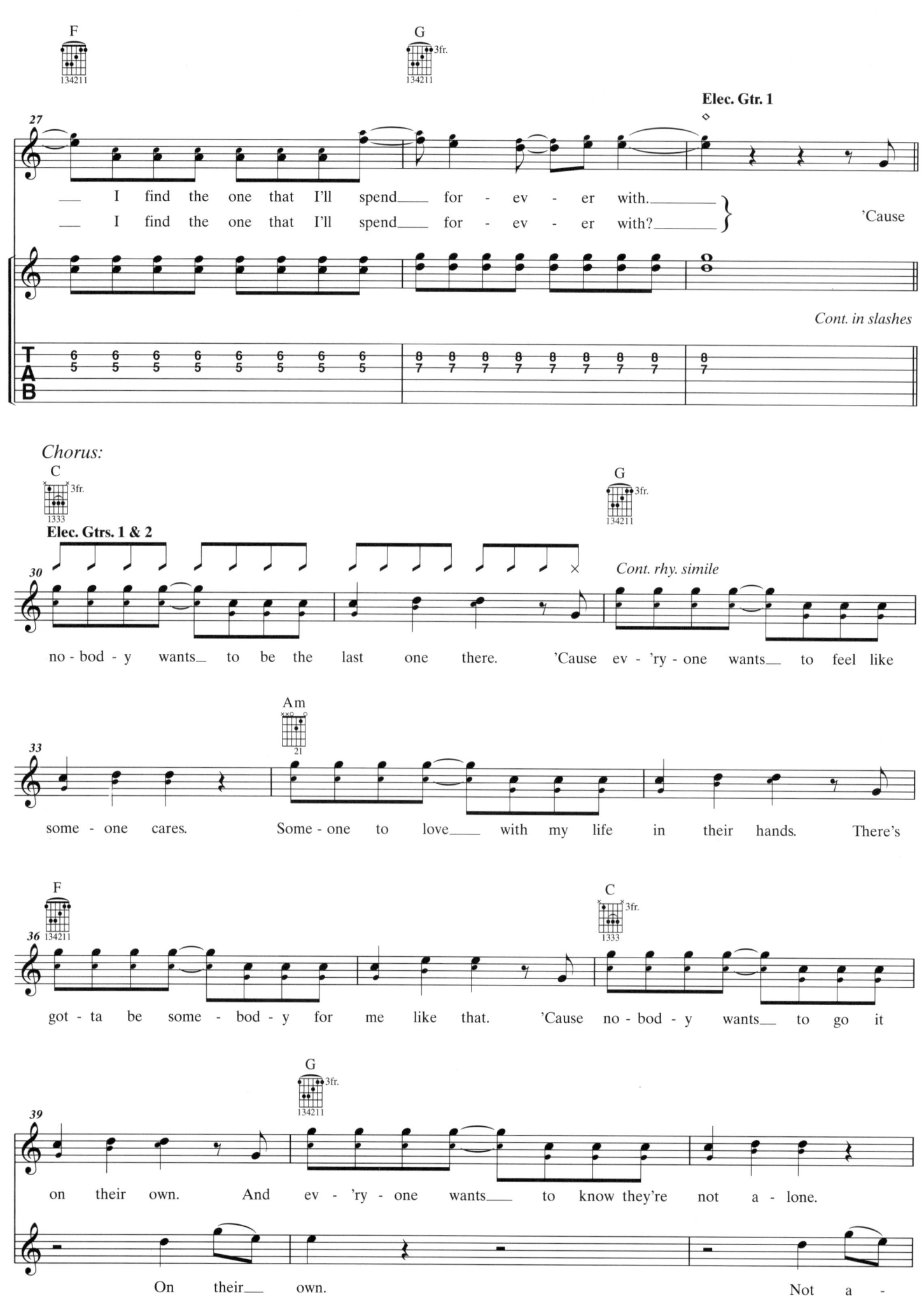

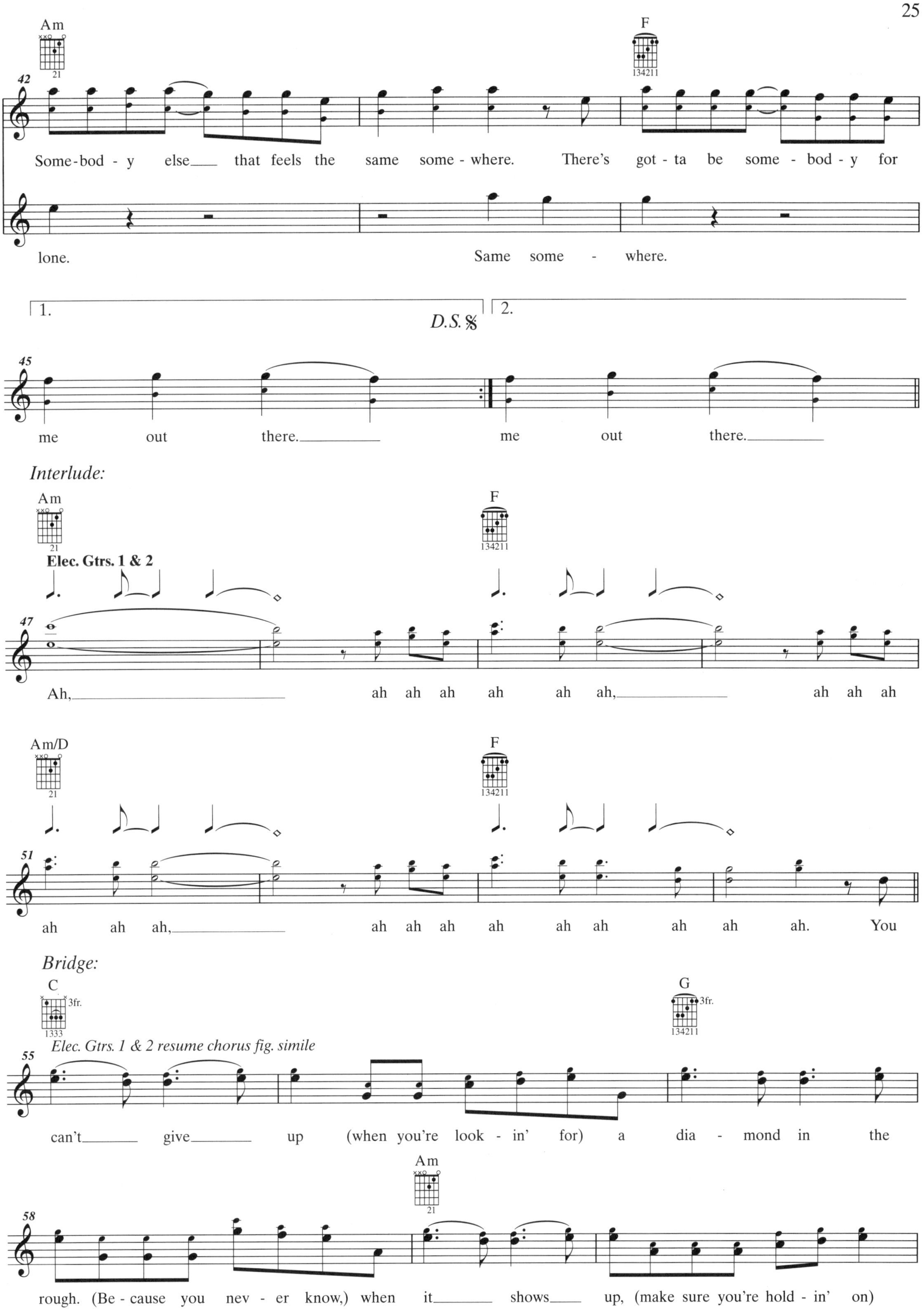
Am
F
42
Some-bod - y else___ that feels the same some - where. There's got - ta be some - bod - y for
lone. Same some - where.
1.
D.S. 𝄋
2.
45
me out there.______ me out there.______
Interlude:
Am
F
Elec. Gtrs. 1 & 2
47
Ah,______ ah ah ah ah ah ah,______ ah ah ah
Am/D
F
51
ah ah ah,______ ah ah ah ah ah ah ah ah ah. You
Bridge:
C
3fr.
G
3fr.
Elec. Gtrs. 1 & 2 resume chorus fig. simile
55
can't______ give______ up (when you're look - in' for) a dia - mond in the
Am
58
rough. (Be - cause you nev - er know,) when it______ shows___ up, (make sure you're hold - in' on)

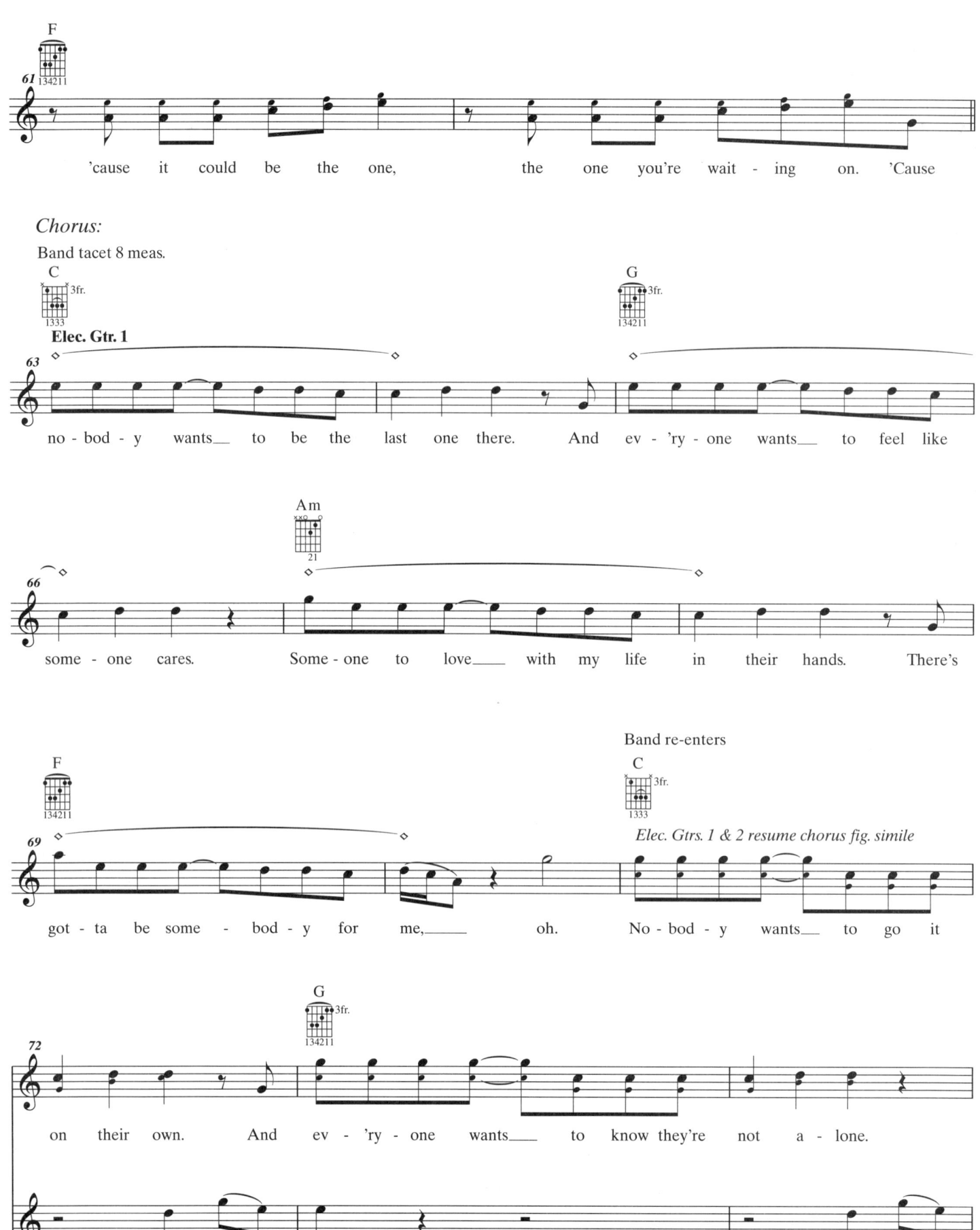

I'D COME FOR YOU

Words and Music by
CHAD KROEGER and MUTT LANGE

© 2008 WARNER-TAMERLANE PUBLISHING CORP., ARM YOUR DILLO PUBLISHING INC.,
and OUT OF POCKET PRODUCTIONS LTD.
All Rights on behalf of itself and ARM YOUR DILLO PUBLISHING INC.
Administered by WARNER-TAMERLANE PUBLISHING CORP.
All Rights Reserved

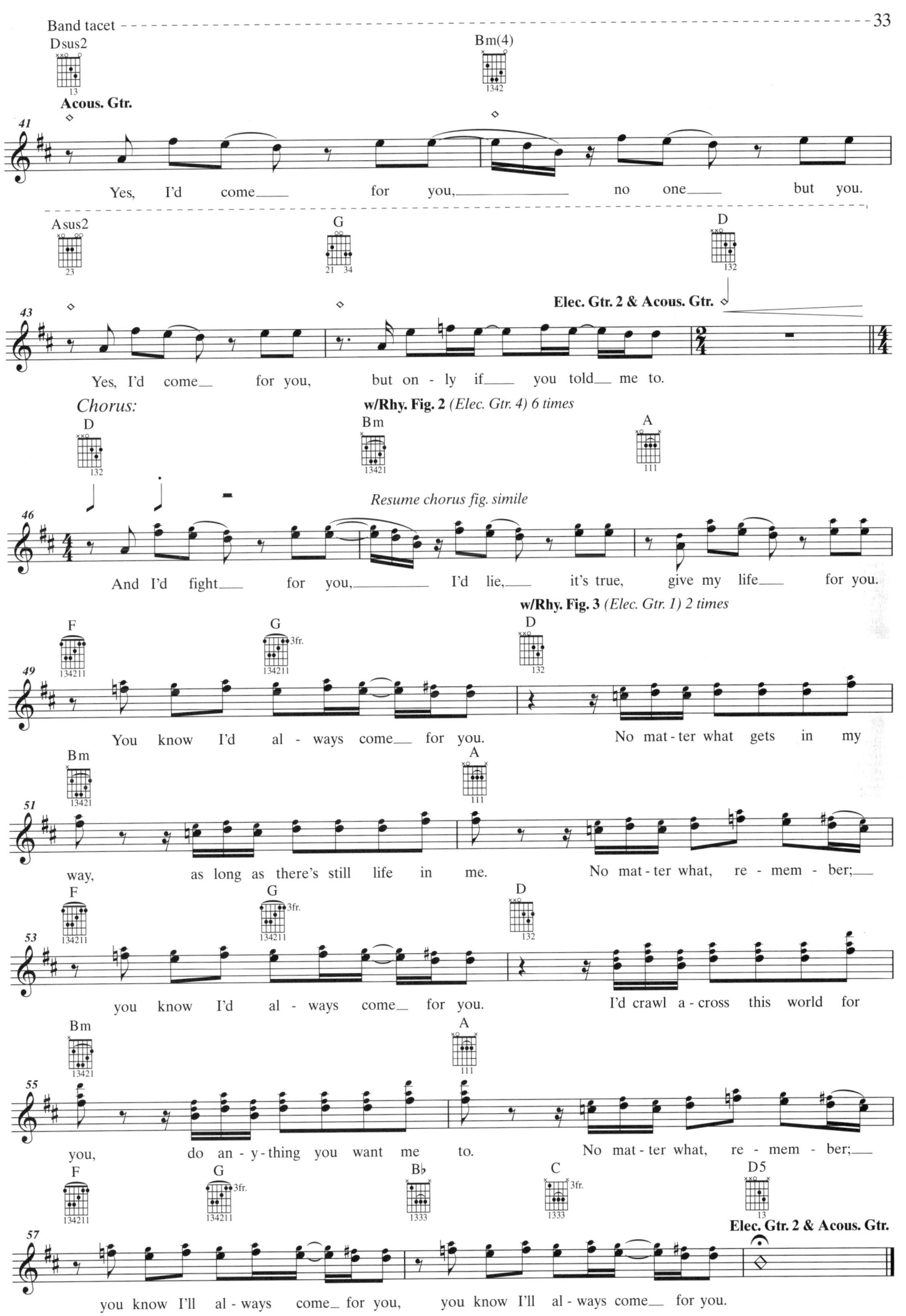

NEXT GO ROUND

*All gtrs. in Drop D, down 1 whole step:
⑥ = C   ③ = F
⑤ = G   ② = A
④ = C   ① = D

Words and Music by
CHAD KROEGER

*Recording sounds one whole step lower than written.
**Composite arrangement.

Next Go Round - 7 - 1   © 2008 WARNER-TAMERLANE PUBLISHING CORP. and ARM YOUR DILLO PUBLISHING INC.
All Rights Administered by WARNER-TAMERLANE PUBLISHING CORP.
All Rights Reserved

40

JUST TO GET HIGH

All gtrs. in Drop D, ⑥ = D

Moderately fast ♩ = 142

Intro:

Words and Music by
CHAD KROEGER

Rhy. Fig. 1
Elec. Gtr. 1 *(clean-tone)*

mf hold throughout

Chords are implied.

(Ah.)

end Rhy. Fig. 1

Verse:
w/Rhy. Fig. 1 (Elec. Gtr. 1) 2 times

1. He was my best friend, I tried to help him. But he traded ev'rything for suff'ring and found himself alone. I watched the ly-ing turn into hiding. With scars on both

2. ing, he gave up eating. He sold his moth-er's rings, she said nothing and pretended not to know. He started steal-ing to supply the feel-ing. Found out he pulled

© 2008 WARNER-TAMERLANE PUBLISHING CORP. and ARM YOUR DILLO PUBLISHING INC.
All Rights Administered by WARNER-TAMERLANE PUBLISHING CORP.
All Rights Reserved

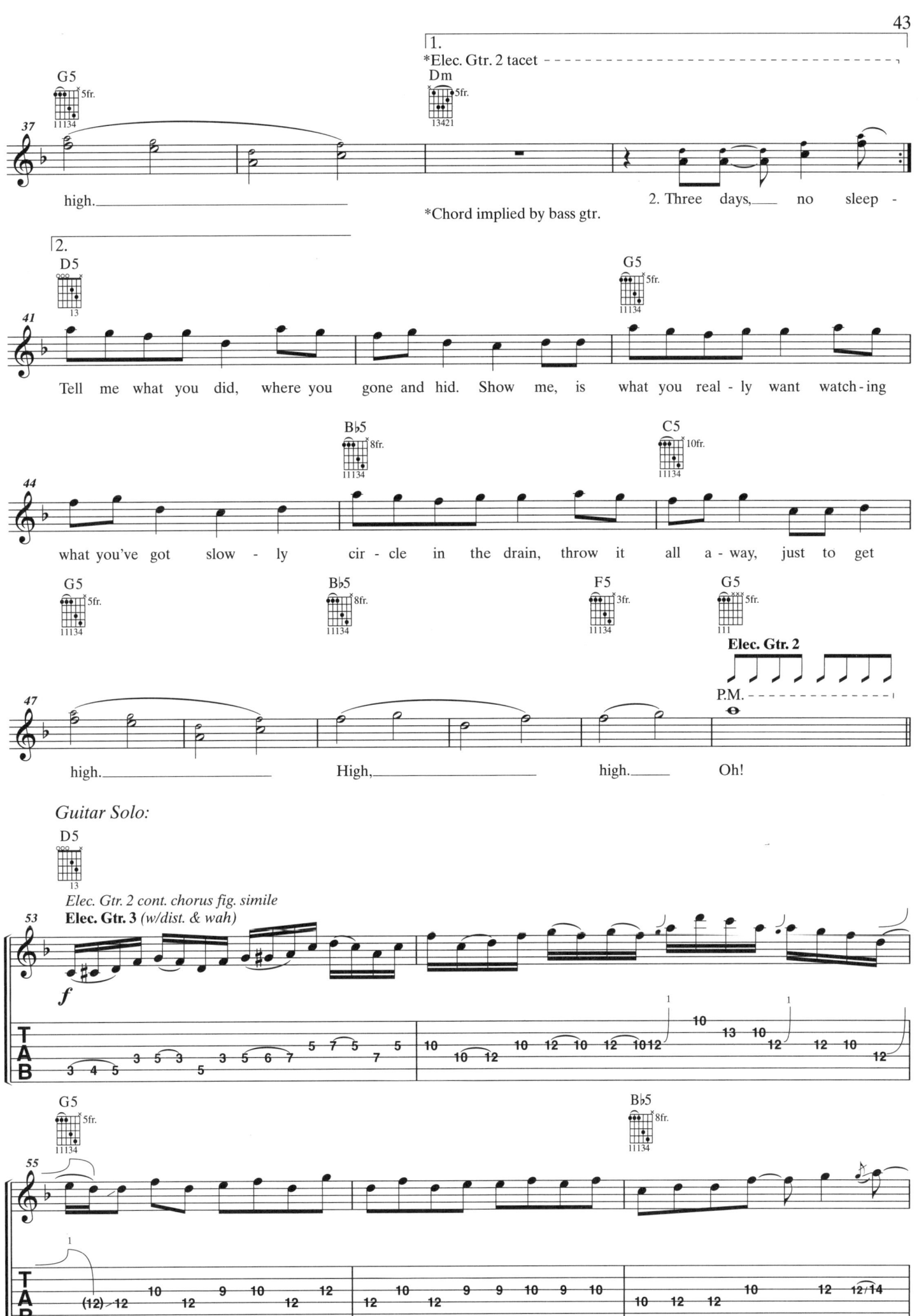

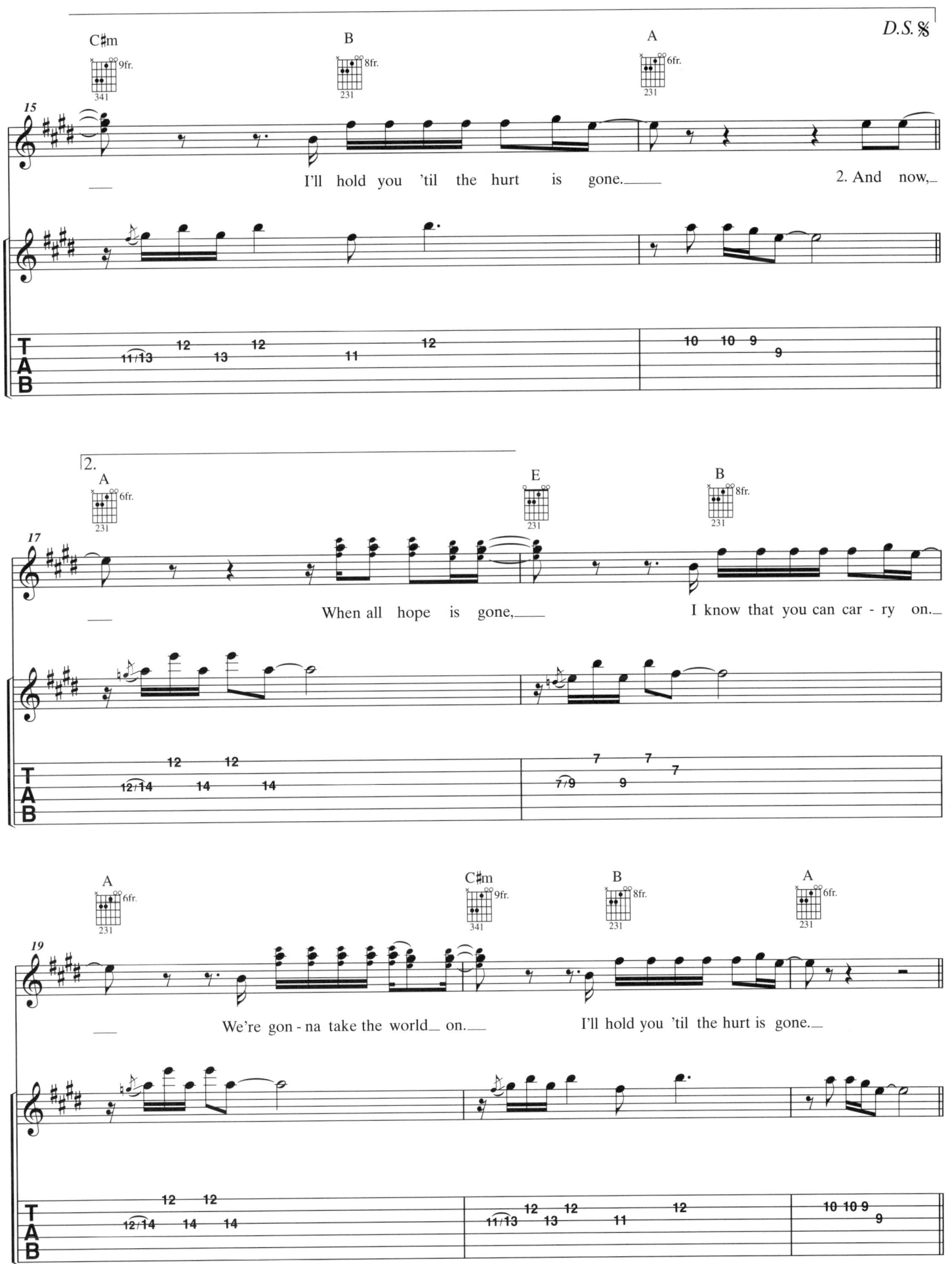

53

SHAKIN' HANDS

Words and Music by
CHAD KROEGER, JOEY MOI
and MUTT LANGE

All gtrs. in Drop D, ⑥ = D

Moderately slow ♩ = 76

© 2008 WARNER-TAMERLANE PUBLISHING CORP., ARM YOUR DILLO PUBLISHING INC.,
MOI MUSIC PRODUCTIONS INC. and OUT OF POCKET PRODUCTIONS LTD.
All Rights on behalf of itself, ARM YOUR DILLO PUBLISHING INC. and MOI MUSIC PRODUCTIONS INC.
Administered by WARNER-TAMERLANE PUBLISHING CORP.
All Rights Reserved

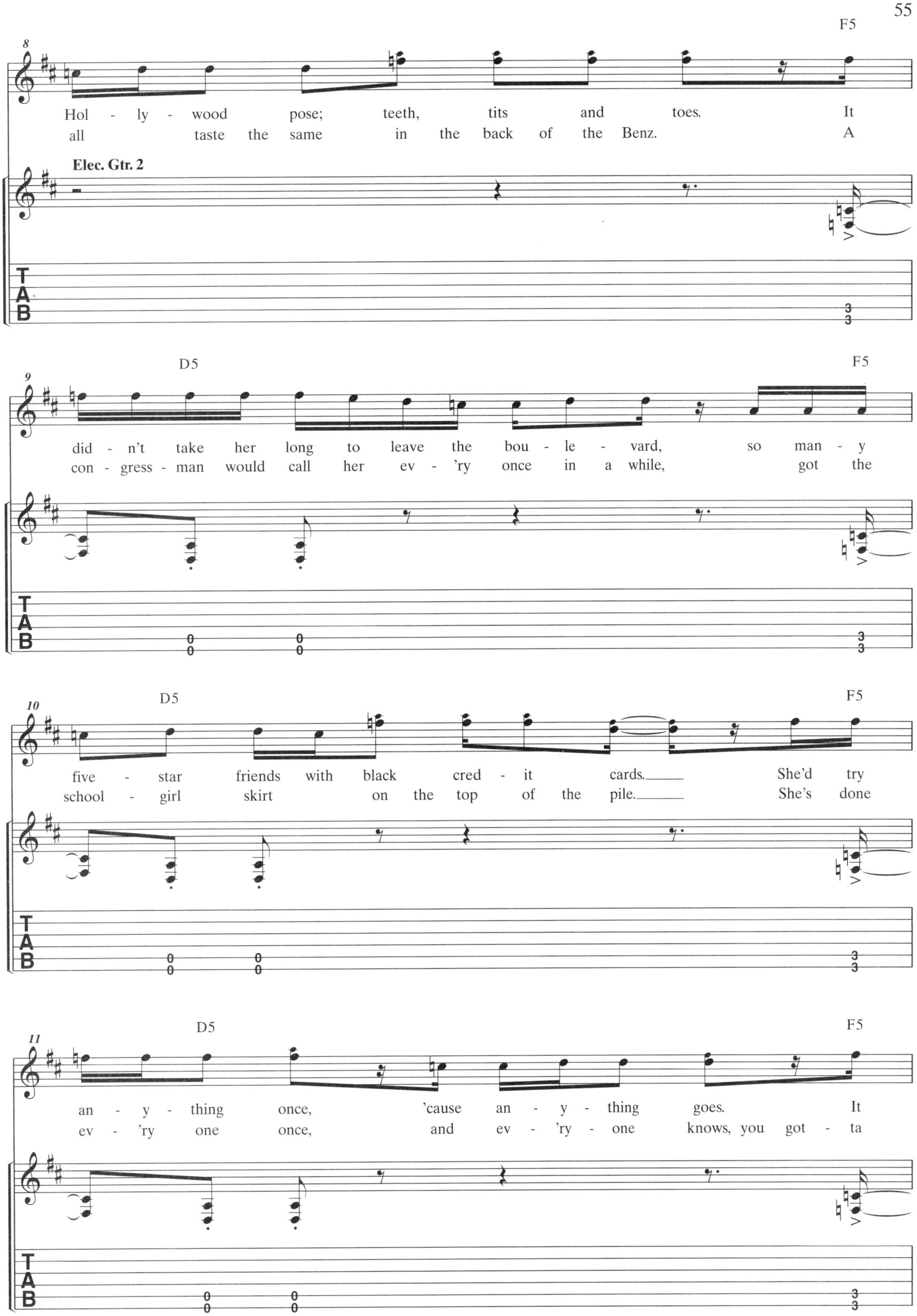
F5
Hol - ly - wood pose; teeth, tits and toes. It
all taste the same in the back of the Benz. A
Elec. Gtr. 2
D5
F5
did - n't take her long to leave the bou - le - vard, so man - y
con - gress - man would call her ev - 'ry once in a while, got the
D5
F5
five - star friends with black cred - it cards. She'd try
school - girl skirt on the top of the pile. She's done
D5
F5
an - y - thing once, 'cause an - y - thing goes. It
ev - 'ry one once, and ev - 'ry - one knows, you got - ta

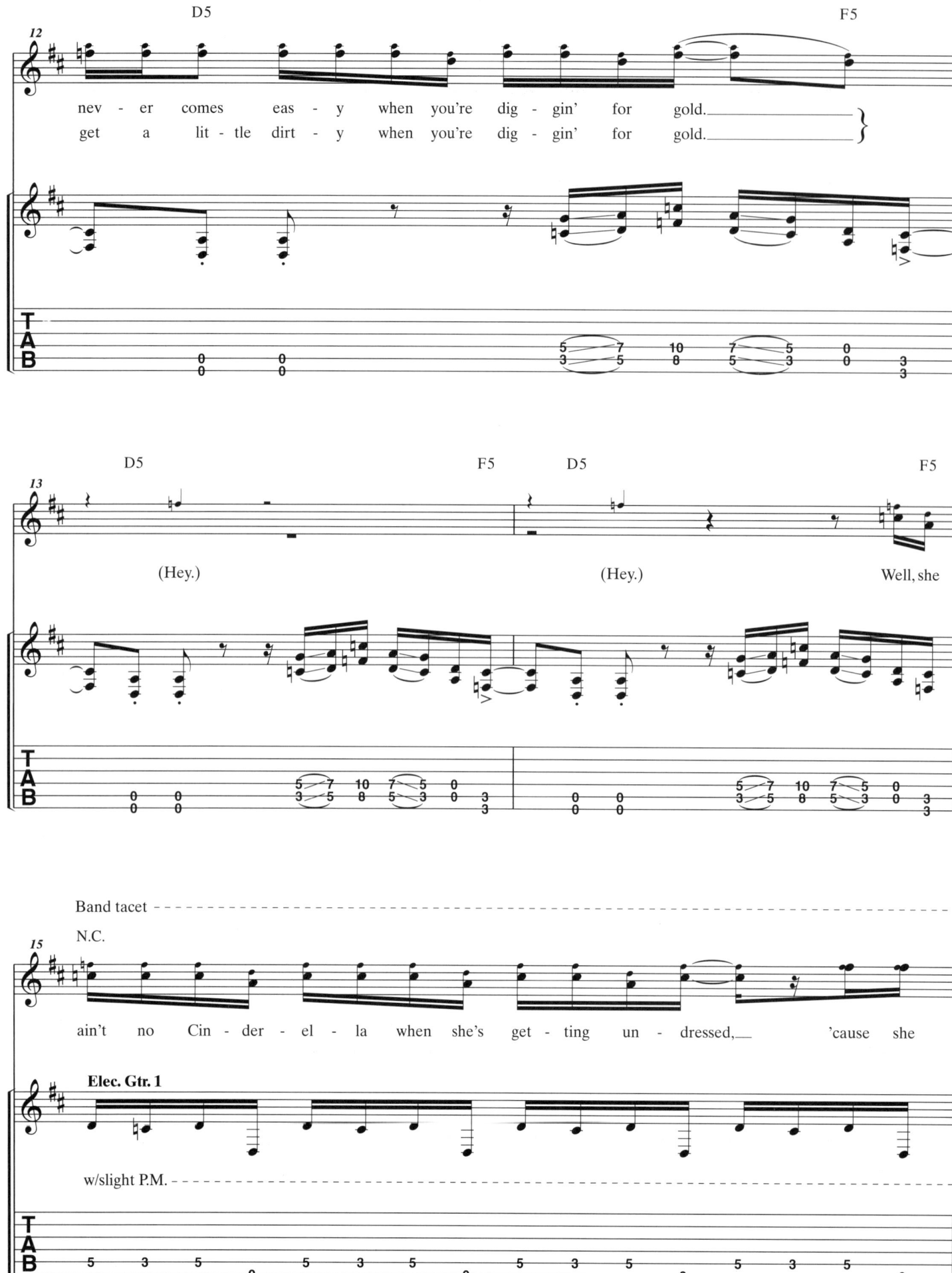

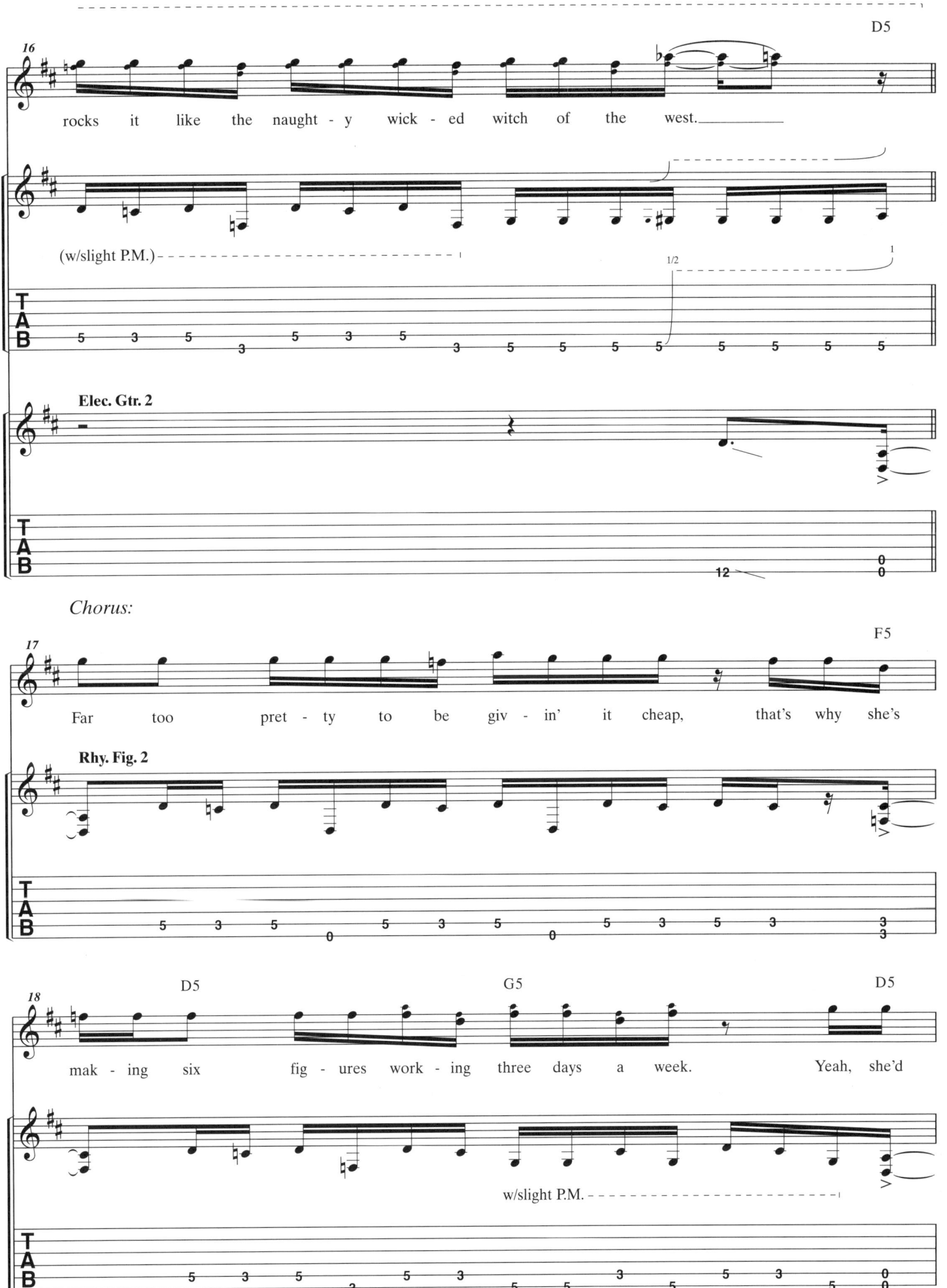

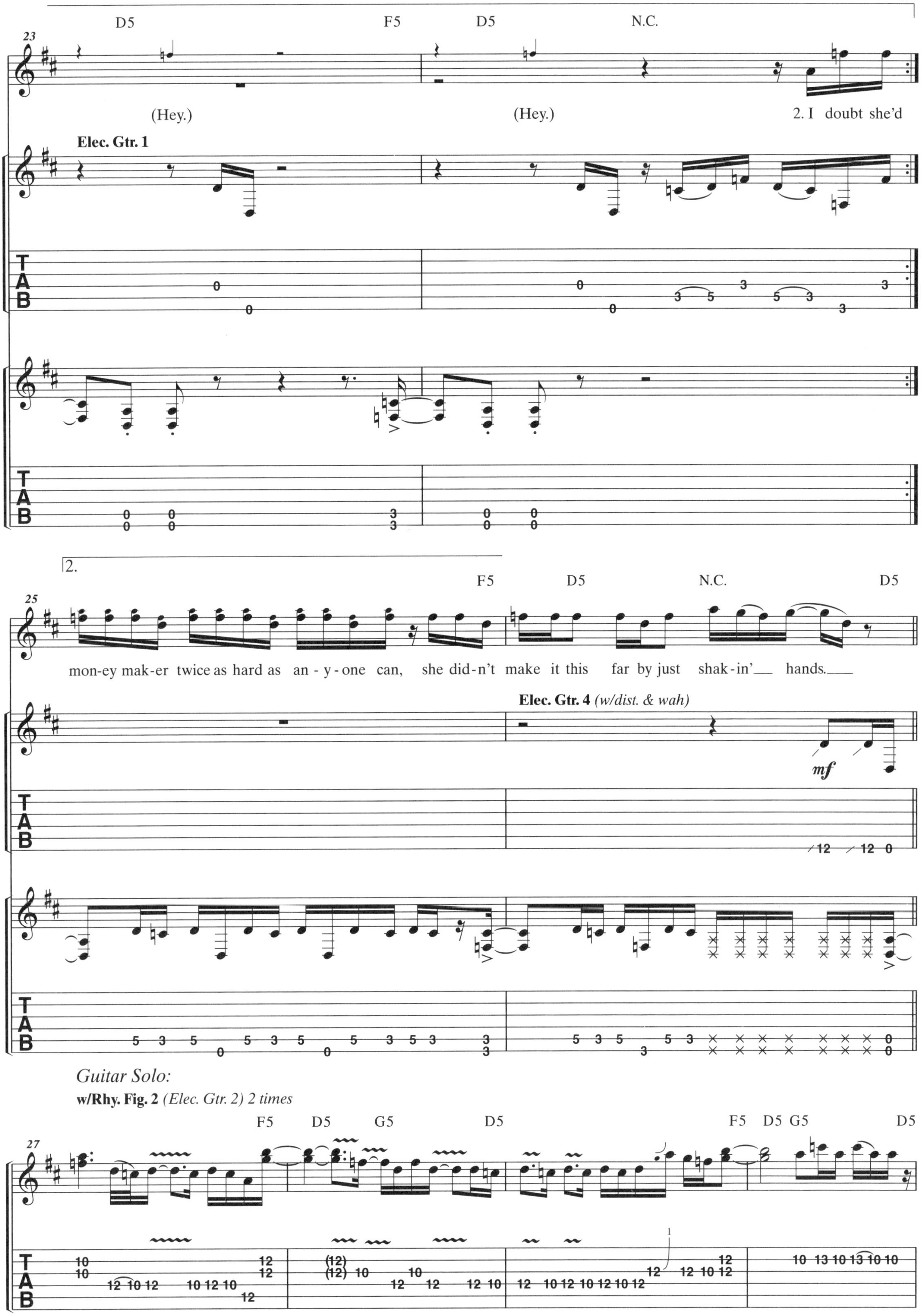
D5 F5 D5 N.C.
(Hey.) (Hey.) 2. I doubt she'd
Elec. Gtr. 1
2.
F5 D5 N.C. D5
mon-ey mak-er twice as hard as an-y-one can, she did-n't make it this far by just shak-in' hands.
Elec. Gtr. 4 (w/dist. & wah)
mf
Guitar Solo:
w/Rhy. Fig. 2 (Elec. Gtr. 2) 2 times
F5 D5 G5 D5 F5 D5 G5 D5

S.E.X.

Words and Music by
CHAD KROEGER

*All gtrs. in Drop D, down 1 whole step:
⑥ = C ③ = F
⑤ = G ②ﾠ= A
④ = C ① = D

Moderately fast ♩ = 136

*Recording sounds one whole step lower than written.

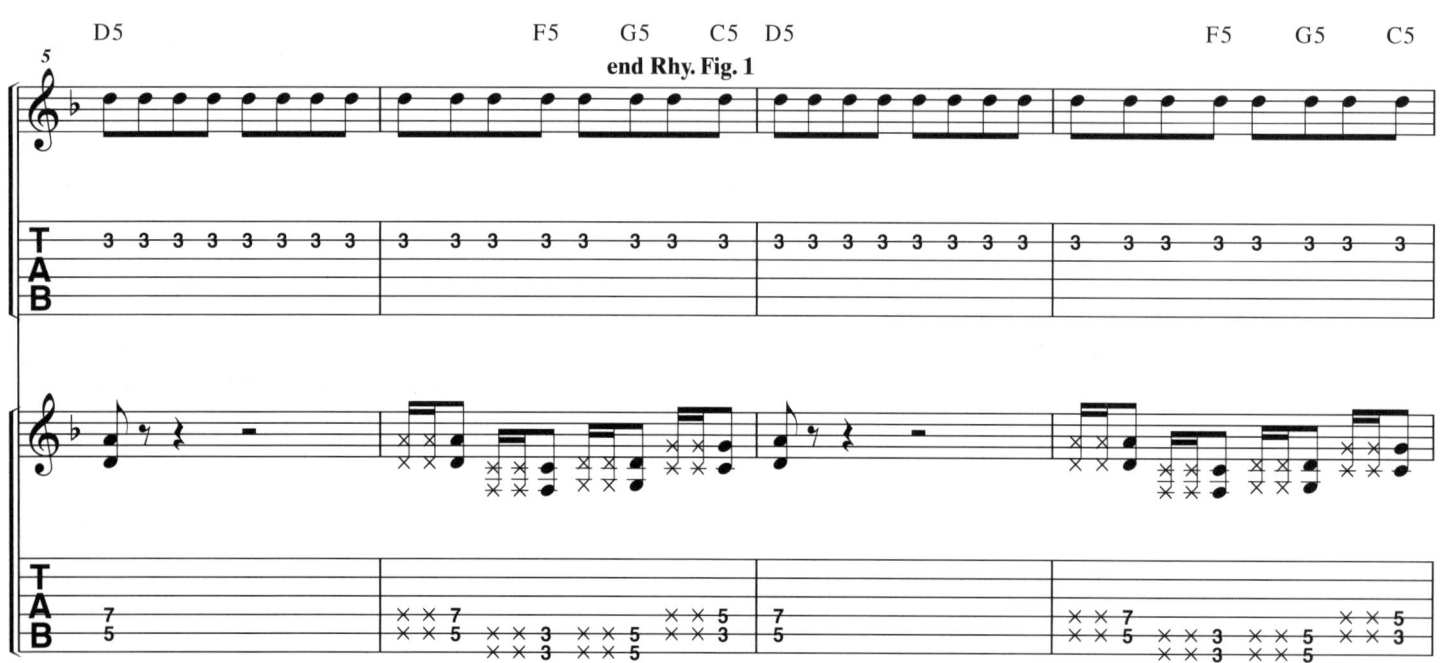

© 2008 WARNER-TAMERLANE PUBLISHING CORP. and ARM YOUR DILLO PUBLISHING INC.
All Rights Administered by WARNER-TAMERLANE PUBLISHING CORP.
All Rights Reserved

If Today Was Your Last Day - 8 - 8

THIS AFTERNOON

Words and Music by
CHAD KROEGER, MIKE KROEGER,
RYAN PEAKE and MUTT LANGE

© 2008 WARNER-TAMERLANE PUBLISHING CORP., ARM YOUR DILLO PUBLISHING INC.,
BLACK DIESEL MUSIC, INC., ZERO-G MUSIC INC. and OUT OF POCKET PRODUCTIONS LTD.
All Rights on behalf of itself, ARM YOUR DILLO PUBLISHING INC., BLACK DIESEL MUSIC, INC.
and ZERO-G MUSIC INC. Administered by WARNER-TAMERLANE PUBLISHING CORP.
All Rights Reserved

This Afternoon - 7 - 6

GUITAR TAB GLOSSARY

TABLATURE EXPLANATION
TAB illustrates the six strings of the guitar.
Notes and chords are indicated by the placement of fret numbers on each string.

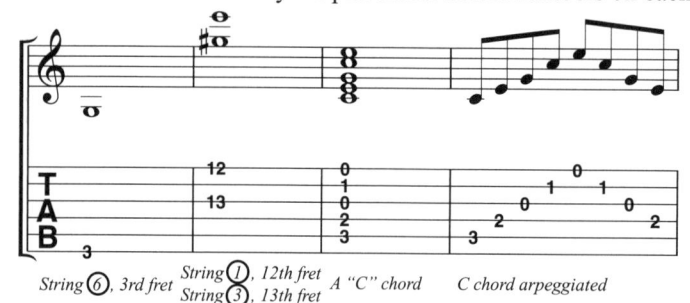

String ⑥, 3rd fret   String ①, 12th fret   A "C" chord   C chord arpeggiated
                 String ③, 13th fret

BENDING NOTES

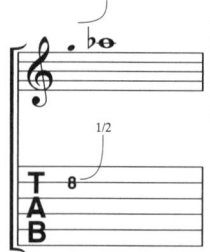 **Half Step:** Play the note and bend string one half step (one fret).

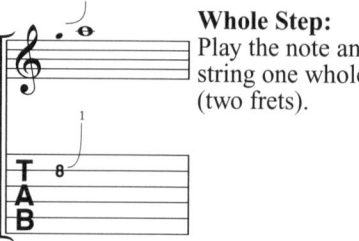 **Whole Step:** Play the note and bend string one whole step (two frets).

Slight Bend/Quarter-Tone Bend: Play the note and bend string sharp.

 **Prebend and Release:** Play the already-bent string, then immediately drop it down to the fretted note.

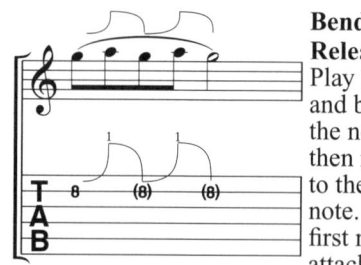 **Bend and Release:** Play the note and bend to the next pitch, then release to the original note. Only the first note is attacked.

PICK DIRECTION

 **Downstrokes and Upstrokes:** The downstroke is indicated with this symbol (⊓) and the upstroke is indicated with this (V).

ARTICULATIONS

 **Hammer On:** Play the lower note, then "hammer" your finger to the higher note. Only the first note is plucked.

 **Pull Off:** Play the higher note with your first finger already in position on the lower note. Pull your finger off the first note with a strong downward motion that plucks the string—sounding the lower note.

 **Palm Mute:** The notes are muted (muffled) by placing the palm of the pick hand lightly on the strings, just in front of the bridge.

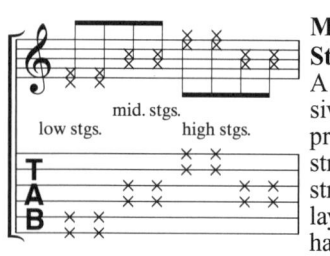 **Muted Strings:** A percussive sound is produced by striking the strings while laying the fret hand across them.

 **Legato Slide:** Play the first note and, keeping pressure applied on the string, slide up to the second note. The diagonal line shows that it is a slide and not a hammer-on or a pull-off.

HARMONICS

 **Natural Harmonic:** A finger of the fret hand lightly touches the string at the note indicated in the TAB and is plucked by the pick producing a bell-like sound called a harmonic.

RHYTHM SLASHES

 **Strum Marks/Rhythm Slashes:** Strum with the indicated rhythm pattern. Strum marks can be located above the staff or within the staff.

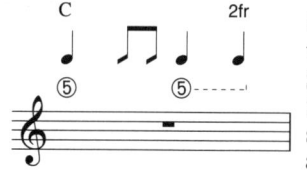 **Single Notes with Rhythm Slashes:** Sometimes single notes are incorporated into a strum pattern. The circled number below is the string and the fret number is above.

 **Artificial Harmonic:** Fret the note at the first TAB number, lightly touch the string at the fret indicated in parens (usually 12 frets higher than the fretted note), then pluck the string with an available finger or your pick.